FAR-OUT GUIDE TO

MARS

Mary Kay Carson

Bailey Books
an imprint of
Enslow Publishers, Inc.
40 Industrial Road
Box 398
Berkeley Heights, NJ 07922
USA
http://www.enslow.com

For Noah George Basso, a future Mars astronaut

Bailey Books, an imprint of Enslow Publishers, Inc.

Copyright © 2011 by Mary Kay Carson

Library of Congress Cataloging-in-Publication Data

Carson, Mary Kay.
    Far-out guide to Mars / Mary Kay Carson.
       p. cm. — (Far-out guide to the solar system)
    Summary: "Presents information about Mars, including fast facts, history, and technology used to study the planet"—Provided by publisher.
    Includes bibliographical references and index.
    ISBN 978-0-7660-3183-8 (Library Ed.)
    ISBN 978-1-59845-185-6 (Paperback Ed.)
    1. Mars (Planet)—Juvenile literature. 2. Solar system—Juvenile literature. I. Title.
    QB641.C3527 2011
    523.43—dc22

                         2009006485

Printed in China

052010 Leo Paper Group, Heshan City, Guangdong, China

10 9 8 7 6 5 4 3 2 1

Image Credits: French Space Agency (CNES) and Los Alamos National Laboratory, p. 39; NASA, pp. 3, 10, 15, 24, 33, 41; NASA Jet Propulsion Laboratory (NASA-JPL), p. 1; NASA, J. Bell (Cornell U.) and M. Wolff (SSI), p. 29; NASA/Greg Shirah, p. 19; NASA/JPL, pp. 4–5, 6–7, 16, 22, 42; NASA/JPL-Caltech, p. 40; NASA/JPL-Caltech/Cornell, p. 20 (bottom), 21; NASA/JPL-Caltech/University of Arizona/MSSS, p. 32; NASA/JPL-Caltech/University of Arizona/Texas A&M University, pp. 34, 36; NASA/JPL-Caltech/USGS/UNM/High-Resolution Science Imaging Experiment, p. 20 (top); NASA/JPL/ASU, pp. 8–9; NASA/JPL/Cornell, pp. 13, 14; NASA/JPL/UA/Lockheed Martin, p. 30; NASA/USGS, p. 11.

Cover Image: NASA Jet Propulsion Laboratory (NASA-JPL)

CONTENTS

Mars

MARS is the fourth planet from the Sun. (Note that the planets' distances are not shown to scale.) It is about half the size of Earth.

INTRODUCTION

Did you know that it snows on Mars? Crystals of water ice—snow—fall from Mars's thin clouds. How do we know this? A robotic lander called *Phoenix* saw snow falling on Mars in 2008. You will learn lots more far-out facts about Mars in this book. Just keep reading!

A PLACE YOU KNOW

Mars seems familiar these days. Pictures of Mars are often in the news and on TV. Most of us recognize Mars's rust-colored, desert-like landscape when we see pictures of it. Mars is a bit like the bottom of the ocean or Antarctica. You know what it looks like, even though you have never been there.

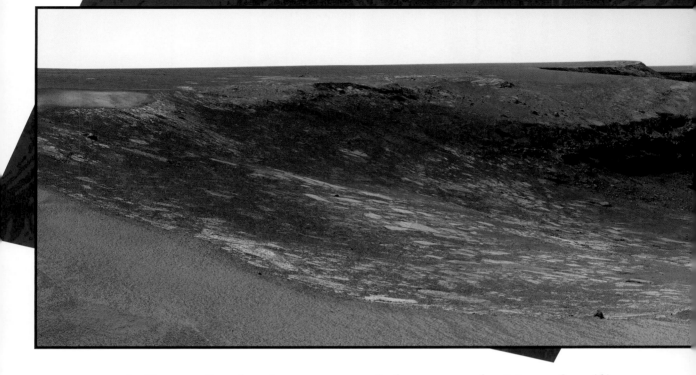

A fleet of robotic spacecraft have made Mars familiar to us. They send back pictures of rocky hills and frosty plains under a pink sky. The Mars Exploration Rovers *Spirit* and *Opportunity* have spent more than six years roaming the planet. And when *Phoenix* landed on Mars, an orbiting space probe photographed it parachuting down toward the surface. Mars is a busy place!

These robotic explorers are the latest of the dozens of space probes sent to Mars in the past fifty years. More will be traveling to Mars in years to come. Today

Mars is a chilly, dusty desert with underground ice and not much air. But scientists believe that long ago Mars was wetter and warmer. Young Mars was more like Earth. Could life of some kind have once lived on Mars? If so, did it leave fossils behind? Do microbes still survive somewhere on the Red Planet? Our neighbor world may turn out to be even more familiar than we think.

FAR-OUT FACT

THE RED PLANET

Mars is often called the Red Planet. The Romans named it after their war god, Mars, because of its bloody color. The fourth planet from the Sun looks reddish, even in the night sky. Mars's red color comes from the rusted iron in its dusty surface soil. Dust in the air even makes the sky pinkish orange.

CHAPTER I

ROCK-
HUNTING
ROVERS

What would a must-see tour of Mars include? Olympus Mons would make the list. It is the biggest volcano in the solar system. Another place is Valles Marineris. It is a canyon system that makes the Grand Canyon look like a ditch. Hellas Planitia is a 2,300-kilometer- (1,400-mile-) wide crater on Mars. Asteroids and comets crashing into the planet created Mars's many bowl-shaped craters.

Mars's canyons, plains, volcanoes, and craters are more than stunning sites. Mars's features hold clues to

Utopia Planitia

Olympus Mons

...ia

Isidis Planitia

Elysium Mons

Amazonis Planitia

...ni Planum

Gusev Crater

Hellas Planitia

THIS map of Mars is color-coded. Mountaintops are white, like the volcano Olympus Mons on the right. High areas are yellow and red. Low areas are green and blue. The lowest places are dark blue, like the giant impact crater Hellas Planitia in the center. The landing sites of the Mars Exploration Rovers (MERs) are marked with red dots. *Opportunity* landed at Meridiani Planun (middle left) and *Spirit* at Gusev Crater (middle right).

a long lost history. They are left from a time when lava burst from volcanoes, asteroids rained down, and water flowed on the planet's surface. Studying the rocks in canyons and craters can tell us what a place was like when they formed—whether on Mars or Earth. Scientists are

THE volcano Olympus Mons is 2½ times taller than Mt. Everest and is as wide as the state of Missouri.

finding out about Mars's watery past by studying its rocks. Two rock-hunting discoverers are the robotic rovers *Spirit* and *Opportunity*.

LUCKY OPPORTUNITY

The Mars Exploration Rover (MER) *Opportunity* arrived on January 24, 2004, at a place called Meridiani Planum. Low, flat plains on Mars are called planums. Scientists

HOW TO STEER A ROVER

Spirit and *Opportunity* are controlled by people on Earth, called rover drivers. It can take twenty minutes for messages from Earth to reach Mars. So the rovers cannot be steered in real-time, like remote-controlled cars. Instead a rover driver must map out the route for each rover on a computer. This gives the driver a "rover eye" view of the nearby terrain on Mars. Once a safe route is mapped out, the driver sends specific instructions to the rover. These tell it how to safely travel the planned route—such as, "move three meters ahead, then turn left."

think that water once covered Mars's low plains. The MER team sent *Opportunity* to Meridiani Planum because an orbiting space probe had spotted hematite there. Hematite is a dark mineral that usually forms in watery places, like seas, lakes, or hot springs.

"It was a gamble," admitted Steve Squyres. He is the scientist in charge of the MER mission. "But we had a hint, visible from orbit, that this was a place where water might have once been." Fortunately for the MER team, *Opportunity* was one lucky rover. The spacecraft that set it down on Mars, its lander, put *Opportunity* in a perfect place. "[W]e rolled right into a little 20-meter [65-foot] impact crater," said Squyres. Craters are great places to look for clues to a planet's past. They are blasted-out holes that reveal buried layers of rock. Those rocks hold a record of what Meridiani Planum was like long ago.

AS *Opportunity* drives away, it looks back and sees its lander. The airbags that once surrounded the lander have deflated. They bounced and rolled *Opportunity* into this crater. Can you see all the rover tracks in the sand?

OPPORTUNITY discovered these hematite balls near its landing site. The circle is where the rover's scraping tool brushed the surface rock to study it better. The tool is called a RAT. It stands for Rock Abrasion Tool.

Opportunity studied the crater's rocks. Right away it discovered something new. The first microscope picture it took of nearby soil showed odd, tiny round things. When *Opportunity* roved over to the crater wall it saw them there, too. The balls of hard mineral were stuck in the rock, "like blueberries in a muffin," said Squyres. The Martian "blueberries" turned out to be mostly hematite. *Opportunity* had found the mineral that hints at Meridiani Planum's wet past.

SPACE scientist and Mars expert Steve Squyres stands next to a full-sized model of a Mars Exploration Rover. Squyres is the scientist that dreamed up *Spirit* and *Opportunity* and heads up their Mars mission.

ARMED AND RAT READY

The Mars Exploration Rovers carried an armload of tools to Mars. Each rover has a robotic arm that can stretch out to study a specific rock. Rover drivers on Earth control where the arm goes. On the end of the arm is a microscopic camera, for taking up-close pictures. There is also a rock abrasion tool (RAT) on the arm. The RAT can drill, grind, or brush rocks to study what is underneath the dusty surface. Another instrument on the arm figures out the kinds of minerals in the rocks.

Opportunity also had tools on its arm. They could grind, drill, and study other rocks in the crater. What did it find? Rock layers with signs that water once flowed there. "We think *Opportunity* is parked on what was once the shoreline of a salty sea on Mars," Steve Squyres told reporters.

The rover then headed off to explore bigger, deeper craters. *Opportunity* went down inside Endurance crater in 2004 and Victoria crater in 2007. The deeper the crater, the older the rocks at its bottom. *Opportunity* found evidence that Meridiani Planum had been wet for hundreds of thousands (maybe millions) of years. "[T]he deeper rocks had been soaked in water for a long time," said Squyres.

UNDEFEATABLE SPIRIT

Halfway around the planet, *Spirit* was trying to make up for lost time. The rover had landed on Mars three weeks before *Opportunity*. But it had been less lucky. It landed in Gusev Crater, a crater with a dry riverbed going into it. "We went to Gusev hoping to find ancient lake-bed deposits," said Squyres. *Spirit* found no such rocks during

MARTIAN MOON ECLIPSES

Spirit and *Opportunity* used their cameras to study more than just rocks. They also photographed dust storms, whirlwinds, the Martian sky and the Sun through the seasons, and Mars's moons. Mars has two small moons, Phobos and Deimos. The rovers photographed both moons as they passed in front of, or eclipsed, the Sun. Scientists studied the orbits of the moons from the photographs. They were the first images of an eclipse on another planet.

months of searching. Gusev Crater was full of volcanic rocks instead. "Mars had sort of faked us out."

The MER team decided to risk sending *Spirit* toward the distant Columbia Hills. There were more interesting rocks there, if the rover could make it. It would take *Spirit* longer to get there than the rover was built to last. Plus one of its wheels was acting up—and winter was coming. Mars spins on a tilt, like Earth, so it has seasons. Winter brings shorter days and less sunlight. *Spirit* and *Opportunity* are solar-powered. Without enough sunlight, they die.

Spirit turned out to be a tough little rover. It reached the Columbia Hills. Then it climbed them! *Spirit* drove across the hilly slopes. This kept it tilted toward the Sun so its solar panels soaked up more energy. As it climbed, *Spirit* studied the rocks around it. It drilled, scraped, and photographed them. What did it find? More evidence of a once water-soaked landscape. After months of climbing, *Spirit* reached a summit called Husband Hill. The rover looked all around, sending back views from

SCIENTISTS believe that millions of years ago Mars was a warmer and wetter world. This illustration shows what both sides of a watery Mars might have once looked like. Can you find some of Mars's famous features, including a flooded Valles Marineris and Hellas Planitia?

SPIRIT looks toward Husband Hill about 850 meters (2,800 feet) away (top photo). Overhead images taken by the orbiting *Mars Reconnaissance Orbiter* helped rover drivers map out a safe and sunny route for solar-powered *Spirit* (bottom).

every direction. "I thought, gosh, aren't we lucky to do what we do?" remembered Steve Squyres. "We just climbed a mountain on Mars!"

ONCE WET

Spirit's success did not end at Husband Hill. In 2007 the rover was driving along, dragging its now dead wheel. The bad wheel dug out soil as it went, leaving a trench

SPIRIT'S view from atop Husband Hill in 2005. The rover looks toward the north, down into the sandy drifts and rocky outcrops of the "Tennessee Valley."

behind it. When MER scientists looked at *Spirit*'s pictures, they saw something unbelievable. Some soil in the bottom of one of the trenches was as bright as white snow. The white, powdery soil turned out to be a special kind of silica. It only forms in water, often in hot springs.

Spirit and *Opportunity* cannot tell if something is a fossil. But the piling-up evidence of ancient water makes scientists wonder if there could be fossils on Mars. Hot springs on Earth that have the kind of silica *Spirit* found are often full of simple life forms. If Mars once had similar hot springs, microbes might have lived in them, too. "[The silica] is a remarkable discovery," said Squyres. And *Spirit* only found it after nearly 1,200 days on Mars. "It makes you wonder what else is still out there."

FAR-OUT FACT

GOING AND GOING . . .

Spirit and *Opportunity* were designed to last only 90 days. But thanks to some luck and a team of talented engineers back on Earth, they explored Mars for more than six *years*. The rovers got smarter thanks to software upgrades. Strong swirling wind helped to clean off their solar panels from time to time. And engineers practiced new moves— like mountain climbing or getting out of sand traps—on Earth with a test rover before sending instructions to *Spirit* and *Opportunity*.

Mars at a Glance

Diameter: 6,794 kilometers (4,222 miles)

Volume: 15% of Earth's

Mass: 10.7% of Earth's, or 641,850,000,000 trillion kilograms

Gravity: A 75-pound kid would weigh 28½ pounds

Position: Fourth planet from the Sun

Average Distance from Sun: 227,936,640 kilometers (141,633,260 miles)

Day Length (One Spin): 24 hours and 37 minutes

Year Length: 687 Earth days

Color: Rusty red

Atmosphere: 95% carbon dioxide; 3% nitrogen; 2% argon

Surface: Rock

Minimum/Maximum Surface Temperature: -87/-5 degrees Celsius (-125/23 degrees Fahrenheit)

Moons: Two, Phobos and Deimos

Rings: None

Namesake: Roman god of war

Symbol:

Planet Fast Facts

★ **Mars is called the Red Planet because of its color. It looks reddish-orange in the night sky. Its color comes from rusty red, iron-rich minerals in its soil.**

★ **The path Mars takes around the Sun is a stretched-out oval. This means Mars can be as close as 206,620,000 kilometers (128,390,000 miles) to the Sun or as far as 249,230,000 kilometers (154,860,000 miles) away from it.**

★ **Spectacular features cover Mars, including canyons, mountains, volcanoes, craters, polar ice caps, and plains pebbled with boulders.**

★ **The biggest known volcano in the solar system is on Mars. Olympus Mons is a huge inactive volcano as big as the state of New Mexico.**

★ **Valles Marineris is an enormous Martian canyon system 4,000 kilometers (2,500 miles) long.**

★ **The southern half of Mars is mostly ancient highlands covered in craters, while the northern half is mostly younger low plains.**

★ **Mars is about half Earth's size, is 1½ times farther from the Sun, and gets less than half the sunlight Earth does.**

★ **Mars is a cold desert world with little air.**

★ **The average temperature on Mars is about -60 degrees Celsius (-80 degrees Fahrenheit).**

★ **Mars's atmosphere is about 100 times less dense than Earth's.**

★ **The air around Mars is mostly carbon dioxide, the gas we breathe out.**

★ Martian weather includes wind, clouds, snow, winter carbon-dioxide frost, and summer dust storms.

★ Dust storms on Mars can cover thousands of kilometers and last for months. Some years a gigantic dust storm covers the whole planet.

★ Mars spins on a tilt, like Earth, so it has seasons. But because Mars's year lasts twice as long, so do its spring, summer, autumn, and winter.

★ Billions of years ago, Mars had water on its surface. Evidence of ancient seas, canyon-cutting rivers, and once water-soaked environments has been found on the planet's surface and in its rocks.

★ Today no liquid water can exist on Mars, but there is underground frozen water in many places.

★ Mars likely once had an environment that could have supported life. But no definite evidence of past (or present) life has been found.

Moons Fast Facts

★ Mars's two moons, Phobos and Deimos, are both small. Each is less than 27 kilometers (17 miles) wide.

★ Mars's small potato-shaped moons are probably asteroids caught by the planet's gravity long ago.

★ Phobos orbits only 6,000 kilometers (3,700 miles) above Mars—closer than any other known moon.

★ Phobos moves about two meters (six feet) closer to Mars every hundred years. Within fifty million years it will crash into Mars or be torn apart by the planet's gravity.

★ Deimos orbits Mars once every thirty hours, while closer-in Phobos circles every eight hours.

Mission Fast Facts

★ No astronauts have visited Mars—yet. Many believe humans will go to Mars sometime during this century.

★ The travel distance between Earth and Mars varies from about 54,500,000 kilometers (33,900,000 miles) to about 401,300,000 kilometers (249,000,000 miles).

★ Every twenty-six months or so, Mars and Earth are in the positions for the shortest spacecraft route between the two worlds, called a "launch window."

★ Of the forty or so spacecraft sent to Mars since 1960, more than half failed to launch, land, arrive, or stay in contact with Earth.

★ Past and present missions to Mars include flyby probes, landers, rovers, and orbiters.

★ Future missions to Mars may include landers that can drill below the surface, sample-return spacecraft, and above-ground exploring robotic airplanes and balloons.

Mars Timeline
of Exploration and Discovery

(Years given for missions are when spacecraft explored Mars, not launch years.)

PREHISTORY Ancient peoples watch this bright reddish object in the night sky.

1609 Johannes Kepler discovers Mars's somewhat stretched oval-shaped orbit.

1659 Christiaan Huygens makes first drawings of features on Mars.

1666 Giovanni Cassini discovers Mars's ice caps.

1790s William Herschel observes seasonal changes on Mars.

1877 Asaph Hall discovers Mars's moons, Phobos and Deimos.

1878 Giovanni Schiaparelli claims to see a system of lines, or channels, across Mars, which leads some to wonder if Mars is home to civilizations of advanced canal-building beings. (The lines were not actually there.)

1960s A dozen space probes head toward Mars; nine are failures.

1965 *Mariner 4* probe sends back first close-up pictures of Mars. The images of Mars's southern half show a moon-like world covered in craters. Mars seems an uninteresting, dead world.

1971–72 *Mariner 9* studies all of Mars and its moons, taking 7,300 images. The orbiter sees huge volcanoes, enormous valleys, and what look like dry riverbeds. Mars is interesting after all!

1976–82 Twin space probes *Viking 1* and *Viking 2* each put an orbiter around Mars and successfully set a lander on its surface. They study its weather, take thousands of color images, and test soil for signs of life. While the mission is a success, it finds no signs of life, or conditions that could support life. Desert Mars appears dead after all.

1997 *Mars Pathfinder* and its rover, *Sojourner*, study the rocks in the Ares Vallis region.

1997–2006 *Mars Global Surveyor* studies Mars from orbit.

2001 Orbiter *Mars Odyssey* begins mapping the planet's surface.

2003 *Mars Express* begins orbiting Mars.

2004 Twin Mars Exploration Rovers *Spirit* and *Opportunity* begin studying the rocks of Mars, discovering ancient lakes and seas on its surface.

2006 *Mars Reconnaissance Orbiter* begins searching for water on Mars.

2008 *Phoenix* sets down on Mars's arctic ice and discovers soil that could have once supported life.

2012 *Phobos-Grunt* to land on moon Phobos and collect soil to return to Earth after a 2011 launch.
Mars Science Laboratory rover *Curiosity* to begin a two-year search for Martian life after a 2011 launch.

2019 *ExoMars* rovers to explore Mars and drill under its surface after a 2018 launch.

AN illustration shows *Phoenix* on Mars in 2008. It has solar panels for power and a robotic arm for digging.

CHAPTER 2

DIGGING FOR MARTIAN ICE

Liquid water once flowed on Mars and flooded parts of the planet. But did anything ever swim in it? Could Mars once have supported life? The robotic lander *Phoenix* went to find out in 2008. Its mission was to help explore this question: "Is there, or was there ever, life on Mars?" said Peter Smith. Smith was the space scientist in charge of *Phoenix.*

Looking for life-friendly environments on Mars starts with finding water. The chemistry of all known life needs water. Mars is too cold for liquid water today. But underground frozen water is plentiful on the Red Planet. To find some of that ice, *Phoenix* landed near the Martian north pole.

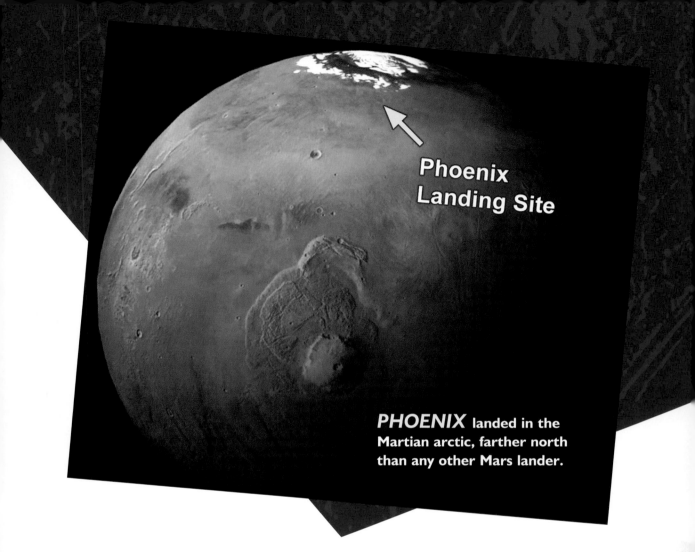

Phoenix
Landing Site

PHOENIX landed in the
Martian arctic, farther north
than any other Mars lander.

AN ICY LANDING

"We landed, looked around, and saw a field of dirt and rock spread out to the horizon," Smith remembered. "We didn't see ice right away and it wasn't until we looked under the spacecraft that we found out we were standing on it." *Phoenix*'s landing jets had blown away the soil covering the ice. "I would bet if you had a broom, you could make an ice rink . . . where we landed," said Smith.

Phoenix soon got to work studying the nearby soil and ice. The lander is a space-traveling chemistry lab. It is loaded with scientific instruments, including a digging robotic arm. "Basically, it works like a backhoe," explained Smith. The arm scoops up soil and dumps it into the instruments onboard the lander. The arm's scoop can also dig trenches down into the ice. "The first thing we saw as we dug one of our first little trenches [was] some

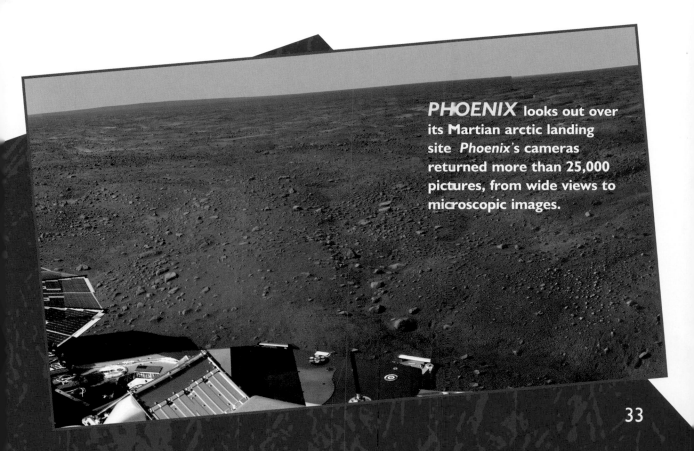

PHOENIX looks out over its Martian arctic landing site *Phoenix*'s cameras returned more than 25,000 pictures, from wide views to microscopic images.

very whitish material," said Smith. Was it a white mineral or salt of some kind?

Within four days the white stuff disappeared. Salt or minerals cannot disappear, but ice easily evaporates on Mars. To be sure what they were seeing was ice, engineers instructed the robotic arm to dump some soil into one of the instruments. It took a few tries to get it to fall out of the scoop. "The soil turned out to be very sticky," explained Smith. Once some Martian soil was finally in

PHOENIX scoops up some soil and gets ready to dump it into the lander's scientific instruments for testing.

WHAT HAPPENED TO MARS?

Mars was once warmer and wetter. It likely had life-friendly conditions similar to a young Earth. So what happened? Both Earth and Mars started out as slushy hot balls when they formed. Mars is farther from the Sun, so it gets less than half the sunlight Earth does. Mars is also half Earth's size, so it cooled down faster. Once Mars's center cooled, it stopped making a strong magnetic field like Earth does. This left Mars's atmosphere unprotected from the Sun's constant stream of charged particles—the solar wind. Larger Earth's stronger gravity helps our planet hold onto its atmosphere better than smaller Mars can. Without a thick blanket of air, Mars cooled even more and its surface water eventually evaporated or froze.

the instrument, it tested positive for water ice. *Phoenix* had become the first to actually touch and taste ice on another world!

GARDENING ON MARS

Phoenix spent five months scooping, sniffing, and tasting Martian arctic soil. Its instruments did soil tests like those a farmer does. It checked the soil's acidity and nutrients. *Phoenix* looked for life-friendly ingredients like nitrogen, carbon, hydrogen, and oxygen. The Martian arctic soil

WATCHING THE WEATHER

Phoenix also carried a weather station to Mars. During its mission it recorded temperature, pressure, humidity, and wind speeds. It also observed haze, clouds, frost, whirlwinds, and even snow falling from clouds. *Phoenix* combined its weather watching with what orbiting probes saw from above Mars. Studying the weather was an important part of the mission. "[Y]ou cannot study a surface in an ice layer without knowing the atmosphere above it," said Peter Smith.

turned out to be not so alien. It had all the ingredients needed for growing green beans! Microbes could live in the soil, too, if they had water and some warmth.

"[I]t's certainly possible that at a warmer, wetter period in Mars' history this could be a habitable zone," said Smith. The Martian arctic could have supported life. The right ingredients are there. But

PHOENIX took this picture of ice in the trench it dug. Scientists watched the ice evaporate over time.

temperatures warm enough to melt ice into water are not. "We think that right now . . . it's certainly too cold for organisms to be alive."

When autumn came to Mars in late 2008, sunshine grew scarce. *Phoenix*'s solar panels could not get enough power to call home. The successful lander was dead. The information and pictures *Phoenix* collected will still be studied by scientists though. "*Phoenix* has given us some surprises," said Peter Smith. He believes more discoveries will be found in coming years as they study what *Phoenix* collected.

FAR-OUT FACT

MARS'S MYSTERIOUS METHANE

Methane is the kind of gas used to heat homes and cook food. Nearly all of Earth's methane comes from life—either organisms living now, or ones buried millions of years ago. When scientists discovered methane in Mars's atmosphere in 2009, many wondered: Is Martian life making the gas? The answer is maybe, but maybe not. Underground microbes on Mars might be making the methane. But it could also be coming from rocks and chemicals mixing underground. The methane could even be left over from ancient volcanoes. It will take more study to solve the mystery of methane on Mars.

CHAPTER 3

WHAT'S NEXT FOR MARS?

The next Mars mission is Mars Science Laboratory (MSL). It is a car-sized rover, named *Curiosity*, set to land in 2012. "Nothing like this has ever been sent to Mars before," said MSL scientist Joy Crisp. Crisp should know. She has worked on Mars missions for more than fifteen years. *Curiosity* is packed with ten science instruments, cameras, a robotic arm, and a rock-studying laser. *Curiosity* is twice as big and four times as heavy as the *Spirit* and *Opportunity*. "Everything is bigger on this rover," said Crisp.

BIGGER, BETTER, STRONGER

Curiosity's mission is to find out whether Mars once had (or still has) an environment that supports

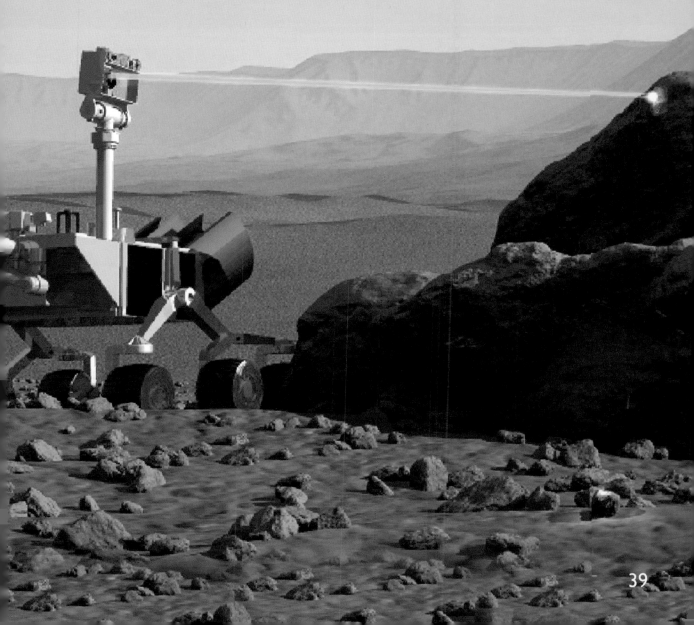

MARS Science Laboratory rover *Curiosity* has a special kind of laser. It can zap rocks and tell what kind they are. Then scientists will be able to decide if they are interesting enough to investigate.

life. Like ice-scooping *Phoenix, Curiosity* will search for evidence that Mars is, or was, a place habitable to life-forms like microbes. But unlike the arctic lander, *Curiosity* will explore a warmer region of Mars. As a rover, *Curiosity* will be able to go over to the most interesting rocks it sees. It is a mobile science lab! And unlike *Spirit* and *Opportunity*, *Curiosity* will not depend on solar panels for power.

ASTRONAUTS ON MARS

Humans might travel to Mars in your lifetime. Sending astronauts to Mars is part of NASA's Vision for Space Exploration. Going back to the Moon around 2020 comes first, however. The idea is that what we learn setting up a moon base will help humans get to Mars by 2050 or so. Would you want to go? It will likely be a two-and-a-half-year trip—six months to get there, a year and a half on Mars, and six months to get back.

It will have its own power generator. The new rover will explore Mars for at least a full Martian year, or 687 Earth days.

Once *Curiosity* finds an interesting rock, it will go to work. Its robotic arm will collect drilled-out bits of rock and dump them into its science lab for study. Onboard instruments will be able to identify minerals and the building blocks of life. Scientists will search the results for evidence of life past or present. "We'll have to put a lot of clues together," Crisp said. "If we get incredibly lucky, we might even see a fossil."

Other Mars missions are also in the works. ExoMars is a rover mission equipped with a large drill scheduled to launch in 2018. After that, space scientists hope to send a sample-return mission to Mars. A sample-return spacecraft would land, scoop up some rocks and soil, and deliver them back to Earth. Studying Martian rocks on Earth is the next big step for scientists. Having pieces of the Red Planet here on our world will likely make Mars seem even more familiar.

FAR-OUT FACT

MARTIAN MOON LANDER

A mission set to arrive in 2012 will not set down in the Martian arctic or equator. It will land on Phobos, one of Mars's two tiny moons. The Russian spacecraft is called *Phobos-Grunt* ("grunt" means soil in Russian). It will set down on Phobos, scoop up some soil, and deliver it back to Earth. Studying a piece of Phobos could tell scientists whether the tiny moon is really an asteroid that Mars captured, like many think. A Chinese orbiter called *Yinghuo-1* will also piggyback a ride to Mars on *Phobos-Grunt*.

Words to Know

asteroid—A large rocky object that orbits the Sun.

atmosphere—The gases that surround a planet, moon, or other object in space.

comet—A large chunk of frozen gases, ice, and dust that orbits the Sun.

core—The center of a planet, moon, or star.

craters—Bowl-shaped holes made by impact explosions from comet or asteroid crashes.

day—The time it takes an object in space to complete one turn or spin.

density—The amount of mass in a specific volume.

diameter—A straight line through the center of a circle or sphere.

evidence—Something that shows or proves a fact.

flyby probe—A space probe that flies by a planet or moon.

fossil—The preserved remains or traces of an ancient living organism.

gravity—The force of attraction between two or more bodies with mass.

habitable—Referring to an environment with conditions that can support life.

hematite—An iron-rich mineral that usually forms in water.

hot spring—A natural spring out of which heated water flows.

instrument—A scientific tool or device.

lander—A space probe that sets down on the surface of a planet or other object in space.

laser—A device that makes a narrow, intense light beam.

lava—Melted rock that comes out of a volcano.

magnetic field—The area of magnetic influence around a magnet, electric current, or planet.

mass—The amount of matter in something.

meteorite—A rock that comes from space.

microbe—A microorganism; a living thing too small to be seen without a microscope such as a bacterium.

mineral—A solid, natural, non-living substance made up of solid chemical elements.

orbit—The path followed by a planet, moon, or other object in space around another object; to move around an object in space.

orbiter—A space probe that orbits a planet, moon, or other object in space.

silica—A mineral found in quartz, sand, flint, and opal.

solar system—The Sun and everything that orbits it.

solar wind—The constant stream of charged particles given off by the Sun.

space probe—A robotic spacecraft launched into space to collect information.

volcano—A break in a planet's or moon's surface where melted rock or gas escape.

whirlwind—A spinning column of air; a dust devil.

Find Out More and Get Updates

BOOKS

Bourgeois, Paulette. *The Jumbo Book of Space*. Toronto: Kids Can Press, 2007.

Carson, Mary Kay. *Exploring the Solar System: A History with 22 Activities*. Chicago: Chicago Review Press, 2008.

Elkins-Tanton, Linda T. *Mars*. New York: Facts on File, 2006.

Fraknoi, Andrew. *Disney's Wonderful World of Space*. New York: Disney Publishing, 2007.

Miller, Ron. *Mars*. Brookfield, Conn.: Twenty-First Century Books, 2006.

Scott, Elaine. *Mars and the Search for Life*. New York: Clarion, 2008.

MARS EXPLORATION WEB SITES

MARS for Kids.
<http://mars.jpl.nasa.gov/funzone_flash.html>

PHOENIX Just for Kids.
<http://phoenix.lpl.arizona.edu/kids.php>

Videos of Mars and Mars Missions.
<http://mars.jpl.nasa.gov/gallery/video/>

PLANET-WATCHING WEB SITES

NightSky Sky Calendar.
<http://www.space.com/spacewatch/sky_calendar.html>

StarDate.
<http://stardate.org/nightsky/planets>

SOLAR SYSTEM WEB SITES

Solar System Exploration.
<http://solarsystem.nasa.gov/kids>

Windows to the Universe.
<http://www.windows.ucar.edu>
Click on "Our Solar System." Then click on "Mars."

Index